SCHOLASTIC

FunnyBone BOOKS

VOCABULARY CARTOON OF THE DAY

180 Reproducible Cartoons That Help Kids Build a ROBUST and PRODIGIOUS Vocabulary

by Marc Tyler Nobleman

NEW YORK • TORONTO • LONDON • AUCKLAND • SYDNEY
MEXICO CITY • NEW DELHI • HONG KONG • BUENOS AIRES

Teaching *Resources*

Cover design by Maria Lilja
Illustrations by Marc Tyler Nobleman
Interior design by Josué Castilleja

ISBN 0-439-51769-9
Copyright © 2005 by Marc Tyler Nobleman
All rights reserved.
Printed in the U.S.A.

4 5 6 7 8 9 10 40 12 11 10 09 08 07 06

INTRODUCTION

Welcome to *FunnyBone Books: Vocabulary Cartoon of the Day!* Cartoons pack more value than many people realize. Good ones require both verbal and visual literacy. The best ones are an inseparable blend of language and image; they cannot be understood if one of those two elements is removed. They're an odd little fusion of puzzle, story, and art. And all this is conveyed in the time it takes to read this sentence.

Best of all, cartoons are funny. Humor is consistently one of the most effective ways to grab people's attention—and improve their memory. We usually remember what makes us laugh. Advertisers know this. Politicians know this. Kids especially know this. As an educator, you must know it, too, or else you wouldn't have read this far.

Some teachers and parents worry that our children have been hit by an epidemic of short attention spans. Whether or not that's true, this book turns short attention spans into a learning tool. However, kids won't see it coming—or won't mind if they do.

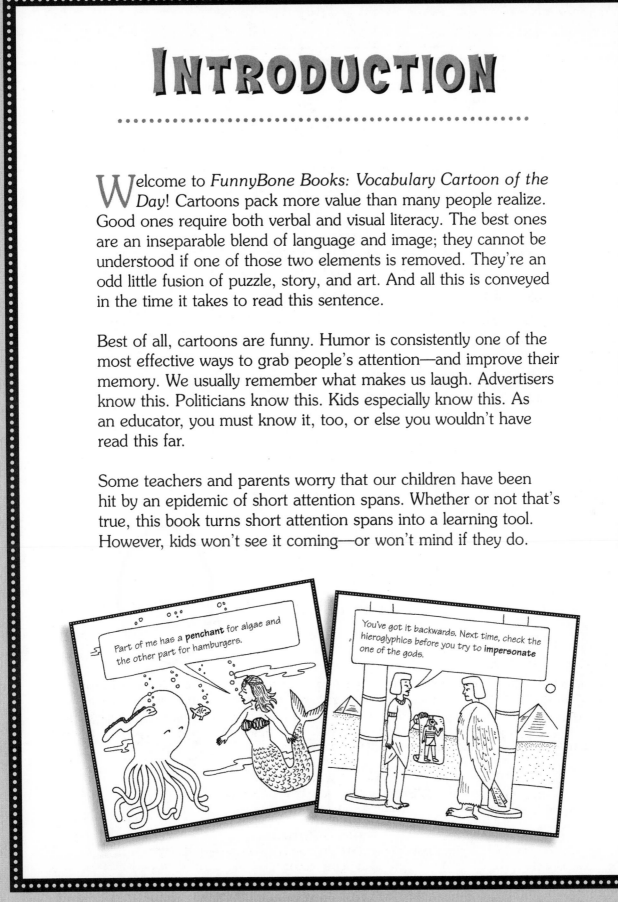

The 180 vocabulary words in this book comprise of verbs, nouns, and adjectives. They're all in common use. Many were gathered from the pages of mainstream news and entertainment magazines that kids will soon be reading, if they aren't already. In other words, this is living language. Though some of the words have multiple meanings, only one meaning is defined, typically the most popular one.

A speaker at a 2002 Society of Children's Book Writers and Illustrators conference said that in 1945, the average schoolchild's vocabulary included 10,000 words. Today, that number has dwindled to 2,500. Ideally, by the end of this book, we're back up at least to 2,680—and hopefully counting.

Welcome to the positive side of short attention spans. It's time to learn by laughing.

1

confound
(verb)

To **confound**
means to confuse or
mix someone up.

> This school map you drew might **confound** our new students, considering it's a school in ancient Egypt.

2

misconstrue
(verb)

To **misconstrue**
means to get the
wrong idea about
something.

> Grandpa, I think you **misconstrue** how e-mail works. You don't need to put a stamp on the computer screen.

A person who is **oblivious** does not know or is not aware of what's happening.

Someone who is **canny** is clever or smart.

overt
(adjective)

Overt means
something that
is open to view;
not secret.

covert
(adjective)

Something **covert**
is not shown
openly; secret.

All you need to do is sit still, look at me, and smile for an **interminable** length of time.

CLASS PHOTOS TODAY!

Interminable means something that seems forever, as if there's no end in sight.

When we built it, we were going more for look than **longevity**.

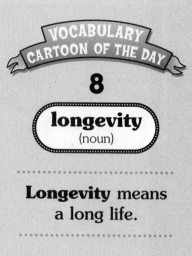

Longevity means a long life.

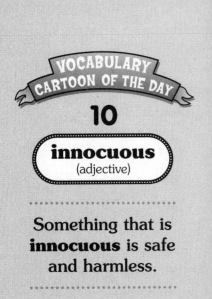

VOCABULARY CARTOON OF THE DAY

9

benign (adjective)

Something that is **benign** is harmless.

Vocabulary Cartoon of the Day Scholastic Teaching Resources

VOCABULARY CARTOON OF THE DAY

10

innocuous (adjective)

Something that is **innocuous** is safe and harmless.

Vocabulary Cartoon of the Day Scholastic Teaching Resources **9**

A person who is
infallible never
makes a mistake.

VOCABULARY
CARTOON OF THE DAY

12

incorrigible
(adjective)

If something is
incorrigible, it is
unable to be corrected.

13

loquacious
(adjective)

Someone who
is **loquacious**
talks too much.

Vocabulary Cartoon of the Day   Scholastic Teaching Resources

14

verbose
(adjective)

Someone who
is **verbose** uses
more words than
is necessary.

benevolent
(adjective)

Benevolent means kind and caring.

Vocabulary Cartoon of the Day   Scholastic Teaching Resources

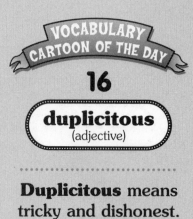

duplicitous
(adjective)

Duplicitous means tricky and dishonest.

excessive
(adjective)

Something that's **excessive** goes beyond the usual limit.

mediocrity
(noun)

Mediocrity is the state of being ordinary or average.

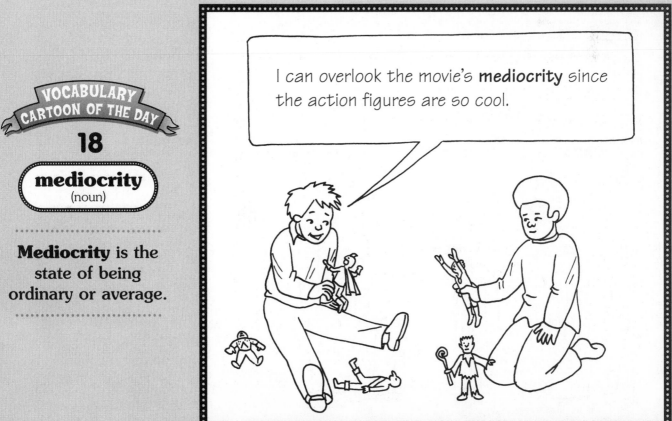

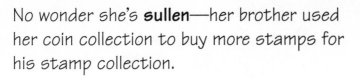

No wonder she's **sullen**—her brother used her coin collection to buy more stamps for his stamp collection.

Vocabulary Cartoon of the Day Scholastic Teaching Resources

VOCABULARY CARTOON OF THE DAY

19

sullen
(adjective)

A person who is **sullen** is sulky or quietly in a bad mood.

I chose him because they say the bigger the dog, the better the **disposition**.

VOCABULARY CARTOON OF THE DAY

20

disposition
(noun)

Disposition means personality or character.

People who **gloat** are happy about other people's failure.

VOCABULARY CARTOON OF THE DAY

22

dispel
(verb)

To **dispel** means to get rid of something by driving it away.

VOCABULARY CARTOON OF THE DAY

23

aversion
(noun)

Aversion means a strong dislike toward something.

VOCABULARY CARTOON OF THE DAY

24

affinity
(noun)

Affinity means a fondness for or attraction toward something.

25

predilection
(noun)

Predilection means a preference for something.

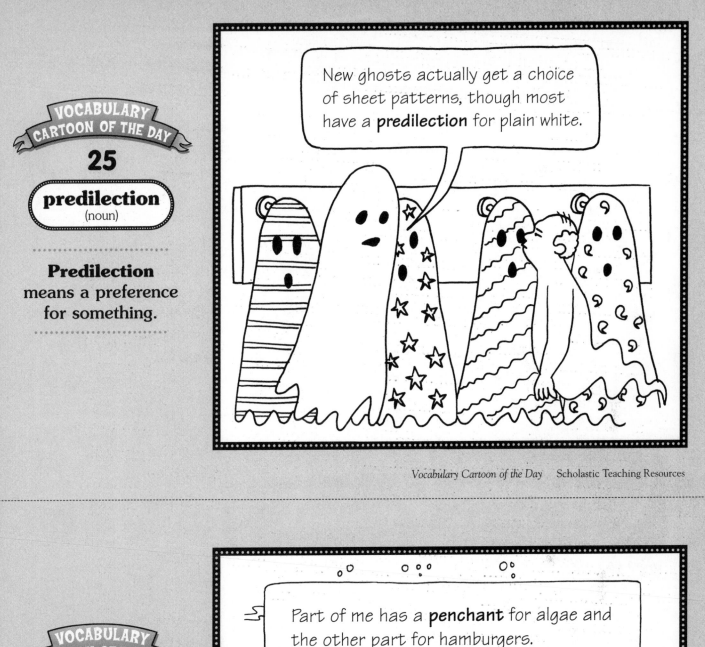

26

penchant
(noun)

Penchant means a strong liking for something.

29

pulchritude
(noun)

Pulchritude
means beauty.

Vocabulary Cartoon of the Day   Scholastic Teaching Resources

30

salient
(adjective)

If something is
salient, it stands out
or is noticeable.

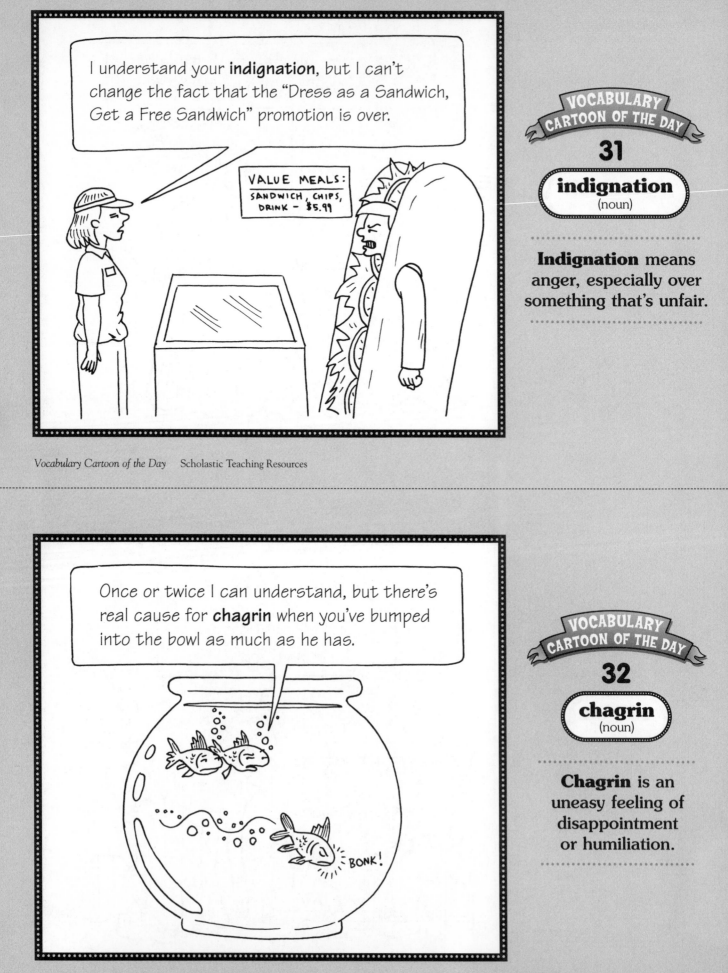

I understand your **indignation**, but I can't change the fact that the "Dress as a Sandwich, Get a Free Sandwich" promotion is over.

VALUE MEALS:
SANDWICH, CHIPS, DRINK — $5.99

Vocabulary Cartoon of the Day Scholastic Teaching Resources

VOCABULARY CARTOON OF THE DAY

31

indignation
(noun)

Indignation means anger, especially over something that's unfair.

Once or twice I can understand, but there's real cause for **chagrin** when you've bumped into the bowl as much as he has.

BONK!

VOCABULARY CARTOON OF THE DAY

32

chagrin
(noun)

Chagrin is an uneasy feeling of disappointment or humiliation.

impersonate
(verb)

To **impersonate** means to mimic or pretend to be someone else.

prodigious
(adjective)

Something that is **prodigious** is enormous or extraordinarily great in size or quantity.

My first few potions weren't **potent**, but I'm starting to get the hang of it.

Vocabulary Cartoon of the Day   Scholastic Teaching Resources

Something that is **potent** is powerful and effective.

This **repository** is only for my eyes of newt! Who put their wings of bat in here, too?

A **repository** is a place or container for storing things.

unflappable
(adjective)

Someone who is **unflappable** has a lot of self-control and is not easily upset or frightened.

stoic
(adjective)

Someone who is **stoic** does not show any feeling, whether it's pleasure or pain.

My diorama may appear to be nothing more than an **idyllic** scene. But those chipmunks are actually plotting to take over the world.

Vocabulary Cartoon of the Day   Scholastic Teaching Resources

VOCABULARY CARTOON OF THE DAY

39

idyllic
(adjective)

Idyllic describes something that's pleasant and peaceful.

I don't want future generations to think we were all **austere**.

VOCABULARY CARTOON OF THE DAY

40

austere
(adjective)

Something that's **austere** looks harsh or severe.

mendacious
(adjective)

Someone who is
mendacious is given
to lying or falsehood.

plausible
(adjective)

Something that is
plausible seems
reasonably true
but may not be.

exploit
(noun)

An **exploit** is a daring or heroic act.

For my next **exploit**, I will bend this steel bar with my bare hands.

MARVO
☆ The ☆
Magnificent
LIAR

Vocabulary Cartoon of the Day Scholastic Teaching Resources

indomitable
(adjective)

Something that is **indomitable** cannot be conquered.

So much for the claim that this mountain is **indomitable**.

SHOP

I want to **instill** in you the belief that you can do anything. Just remember to dress warmly, look both ways, and say "please" before doing it.

47

instill
(verb)

To **instill** means to put a feeling or idea into someone's mind slowly.

This video game is too **didactic**. It doesn't even give your score—you have to add up your points yourself.

VOCABULARY CARTOON OF THE DAY

48

didactic
(adjective)

Something that is **didactic** is designed to teach.

49

demeanor
(noun)

Demeanor is someone's behavior toward others.

Vocabulary Cartoon of the Day   Scholastic Teaching Resources

50

deference
(noun)

Deference means respect for an older or more superior person.

Someone who
is **spry** is
nimble or lively.

VOCABULARY
CARTOON OF THE DAY

52

intrepid
(adjective)

A person who is
intrepid is fearless
and brave.

53

robust
(adjective)

A person who is **robust** feels healthy and strong.

Vocabulary Cartoon of the Day Scholastic Teaching Resources

54

buoyant
(adjective)

A person who feels **buoyant** is happy and cheerful.

My job requires **precision**—one wrong move and I'm advertising the new movie starring Tom Hanky instead of Tom Hanks.

VOCABULARY CARTOON OF THE DAY

55

precision
(noun)

Precision means exactness or accuracy.

Our policy explaining the types of items that are appropriate for Show and Tell is apparently too **nebulous**.

VOCABULARY CARTOON OF THE DAY

56

nebulous
(adjective)

If something is **nebulous**, it is not clear or specific.

57

segue
(noun)

A **segue** is a smooth transition from one thing to another.

58

lapse
(noun)

A **lapse** is a temporary pause or interruption.

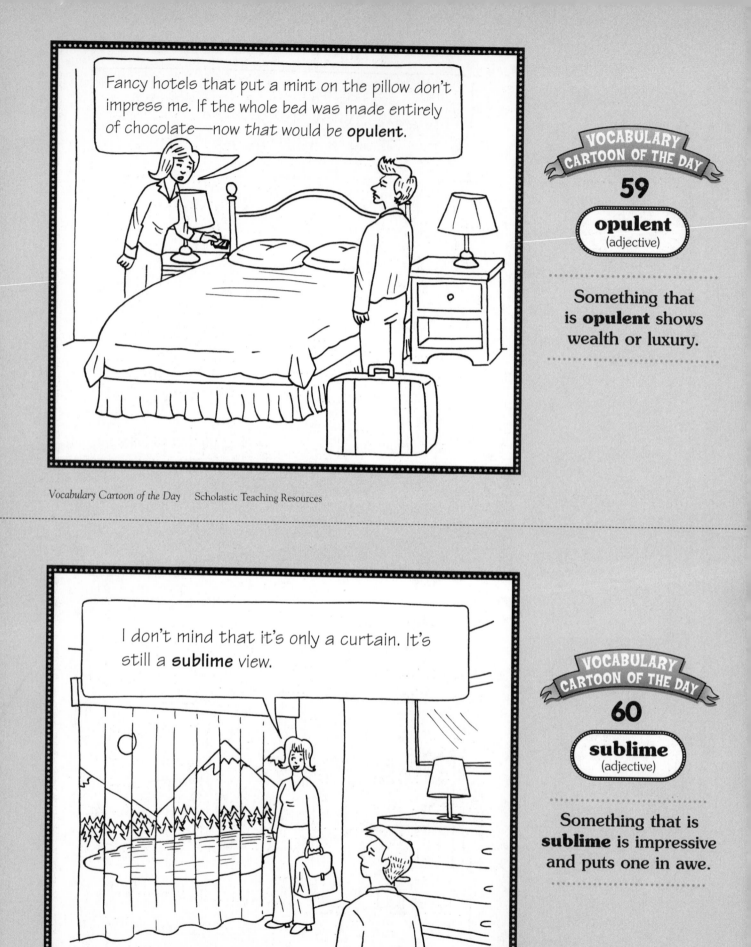

Fancy hotels that put a mint on the pillow don't impress me. If the whole bed was made entirely of chocolate—now that would be **opulent**.

VOCABULARY CARTOON OF THE DAY

59

opulent
(adjective)

Something that is **opulent** shows wealth or luxury.

I don't mind that it's only a curtain. It's still a **sublime** view.

VOCABULARY CARTOON OF THE DAY

60

sublime
(adjective)

Something that is **sublime** is impressive and puts one in awe.

A **mantra** is a phrase that sometimes expresses a major belief and is often repeated.

"Be true and be you" is my **mantra**. "Polly want a cracker" is just something I say a lot.

Vocabulary Cartoon of the Day   Scholastic Teaching Resources

To **reiterate** means to repeat or say something again.

Don't make me **reiterate** it. I already forgot what I just said.

I can **abide** with the bread touching the vegetables and the vegetables touching the meat, but I freak out when the meat touches the bread.

Vocabulary Cartoon of the Day   Scholastic Teaching Resources

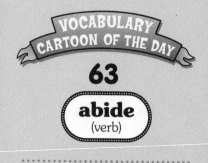

VOCABULARY CARTOON OF THE DAY

63

abide
(verb)

To **abide** means to tolerate or put up with something.

We've only been inside for thirty seconds. How can you be **wistful** for recess already?

VOCABULARY CARTOON OF THE DAY

64

wistful
(adjective)

A person who is **wistful** is longing for something.

If something
is **perennial**,
it is ongoing or
constantly repeated.

Something that is
indelible cannot be
removed or erased.

My parents like to **cull** old photos from our albums and put them on display...but only if they're highly embarrassing.

VOCABULARY CARTOON OF THE DAY

67

cull
(verb)

To **cull** means to pick out from a group.

This sweater would **complement** the pants I just got for my birthday—both hideous, but in the same way.

VOCABULARY CARTOON OF THE DAY

68

complement
(verb)

To **complement** means to match things that go together.

Someone who is **coherent** is clear and easy to understand.

Vocabulary Cartoon of the Day   Scholastic Teaching Resources

---

A **gallant** person is courteous and noble.

VOCABULARY CARTOON OF THE DAY

71

hybrid
(noun)

A **hybrid** is a mix of different breeds or varieties.

VOCABULARY CARTOON OF THE DAY

72

terrain
(noun)

Terrain is a piece of land.

An **impetus** is something that spurs one to move, change, or speed up.

It's been so long since I left that I forgot what the **impetus** was for coming here.

Vocabulary Cartoon of the Day Scholastic Teaching Resources

Culmination means the end result or climax.

It's the **culmination** of lots of hard work— two percent by me, the rest by Mother Nature.

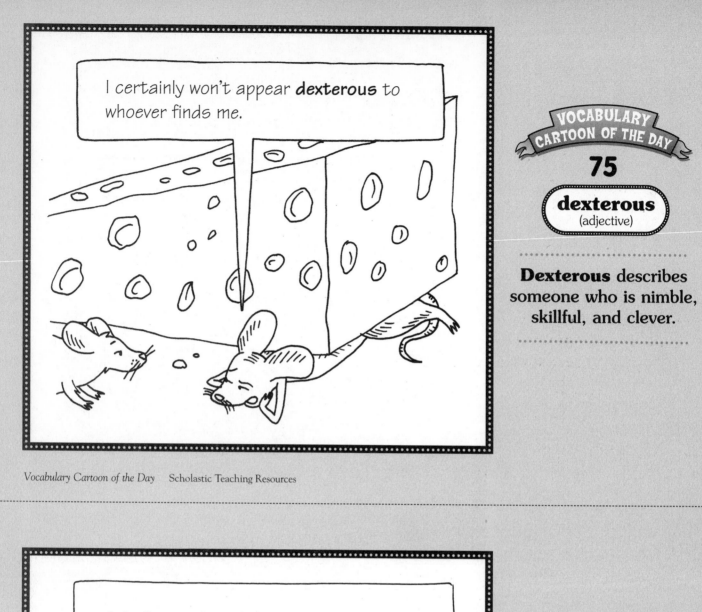

I certainly won't appear **dexterous** to whoever finds me.

VOCABULARY CARTOON OF THE DAY

75

dexterous
(adjective)

Dexterous describes someone who is nimble, skillful, and clever.

I don't speak any other languages, but I am **proficient** in Chinese checkers.

VOCABULARY CARTOON OF THE DAY

76

proficient
(adjective)

Someone who is **proficient** has mastered a particular skill.

77

knack
(noun)

A **knack** is a clever way of doing something; a special talent.

Vocabulary Cartoon of the Day Scholastic Teaching Resources

78

lark
(noun)

A **lark** is something done just for fun.

We may play the worst music, but we **banter** better than any other disc-jockey team in town.

VOCABULARY
CARTOON OF THE DAY

79

banter
(verb)

To **banter** means
to speak playfully
or teasingly.

That was an impressive **harangue**, Michael, but I still don't think the administration will replace the school's water fountains with chocolate-milk fountains.

VOCABULARY
CARTOON OF THE DAY

80

harangue
(noun)

A **harangue** is a
speech delivered with
strong feelings.

81

coax
(verb)

To **coax** means to
persuade gently.

82

coerce
(verb)

To **coerce**
means to force.

Veracity means
truthfulness.

Discrepancy
means a difference
or inconsistency.

It seems like every time we **comply** with a rule, a new one comes along to get used to.

SUNRISE
PARK
RULES
1. No Littering
2. No Flower-Picking
3. No Radios
4. No Entry After Sunset
5. No Skateboarding Without Helmet
6. No Dogs Without Leash

NEW RULE:
No Dogs
Without Helmet

VOCABULARY CARTOON OF THE DAY
87

comply
(verb)

To **comply** means to follow a rule or obey a request.

For the next few years, I'll need some **leeway** to style my hair in a way that may be different than what was allowed in your own childhood.

VOCABULARY CARTOON OF THE DAY
88

leeway
(noun)

Leeway is the flexibility or freedom to do things.

inclement
(adjective)

Something that is **inclement** is severe or rough. In describing weather, it means stormy.

Vocabulary Cartoon of the Day Scholastic Teaching Resources

bamboozle
(verb)

To **bamboozle** means to trick or deceive.

It's only on February 2nd that I use my shadow to **prognosticate**. All other times I prefer more conventional methods.

VOCABULARY CARTOON OF THE DAY

91

prognosticate
(verb)

To **prognosticate** means to predict the future.

I **envision** a day when the world will finally be at peace. We might even get out of school early.

VOCABULARY CARTOON OF THE DAY

92

envision
(verb)

To **envision** means to imagine or picture something in one's head.

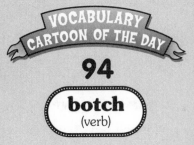

VOCABULARY CARTOON OF THE DAY

93

finesse
(noun)

Finesse is the ability to handle a delicate situation.

Not every fairy has the **finesse** to fly, get the tooth from under the pillow, and leave a quarter without waking the child. What makes you think you're right for this job?

TOOTH FAIRY INTERVIEWS HERE

Vocabulary Cartoon of the Day   Scholastic Teaching Resources

VOCABULARY CARTOON OF THE DAY

94

botch
(verb)

To **botch** something means to do something badly or mess it up.

Now we know that it is possible to **botch** a snowman.

Moving to Hawaii is exciting, but it's only fair to warn you: the number of school snow cancellations will drastically **subside**.

VOCABULARY CARTOON OF THE DAY

95

subside
(verb)

To **subside** means to decrease or become less.

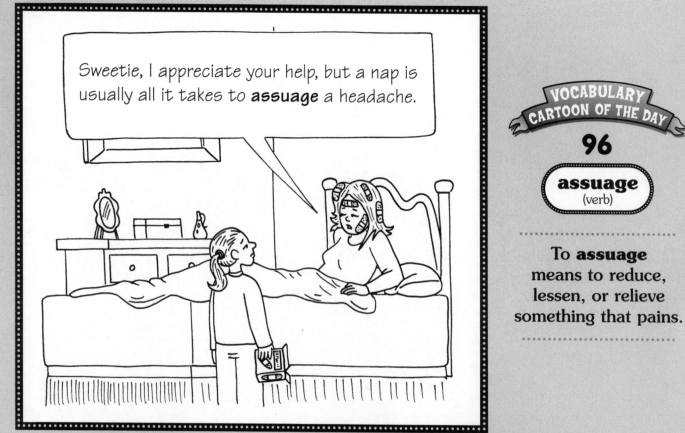

Sweetie, I appreciate your help, but a nap is usually all it takes to **assuage** a headache.

VOCABULARY CARTOON OF THE DAY

96

assuage
(verb)

To **assuage** means to reduce, lessen, or relieve something that pains.

97

deter
(verb)

To **deter** means
to discourage
or prevent.

Let's see if this will **deter** kids from drinking too much soda.

SODA

TOOTH-BRUSHES

98

eschew
(verb)

To **eschew** means
to avoid something.

Until we know if it's friendly, let's **eschew** making eye contact.

101

discern
(verb)

To **discern**
means to detect
or recognize.

We haven't been able to **discern** any microscopic life up here.

102

inkling
(noun)

An **inkling** is a
slight clue or hint.

I have an **inkling** that we're boarding alphabetically.

FORM LINE HERE
FOR NOAH'S ARK

camaraderie
(noun)

Camaraderie means
a spirit of friendship,
especially in a group.

Vocabulary Cartoon of the Day   Scholastic Teaching Resources

comprise
(verb)

To **comprise**
means to consist of
or to include.

console
(verb)

To **console** means to comfort or help someone feel less upset.

contemplate
(verb)

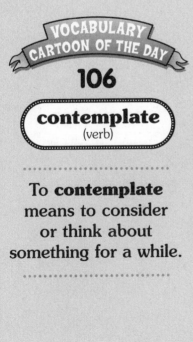

To **contemplate** means to consider or think about something for a while.

This book is so **prosaic** that I'd rather read the owner's manual for a vacuum cleaner.

Vocabulary Cartoon of the Day   Scholastic Teaching Resources

VOCABULARY CARTOON OF THE DAY

107

prosaic
(adjective)

Something that is **prosaic** is dull and unimaginative.

In my house, we divvy up kitchen responsibilities. My parents cook and clean, and I **embellish** the fridge door.

VOCABULARY CARTOON OF THE DAY

108

embellish
(verb)

To **embellish** means to make something more beautiful by decorating it.

flourish
(verb)

To **flourish**
means to thrive or
grow successfully.

exacerbate
(verb)

To **exacerbate**
means to make
things worse.

If I'm having a hard day, why should I have to wait till I get home to **immerse** myself in a warm bath?

VOCABULARY CARTOON OF THE DAY

111

immerse
(verb)

To **immerse** means to plunge into something (often water) and be covered completely.

I'm bored with water. Think we'll ever get a chance to **imbibe** anything else?

VOCABULARY CARTOON OF THE DAY

112

imbibe
(verb)

To **imbibe** means to drink.

preliminary
(adjective)

Something that is **preliminary** is introductory or opening for something else.

brink
(noun)

Brink means edge or verge.

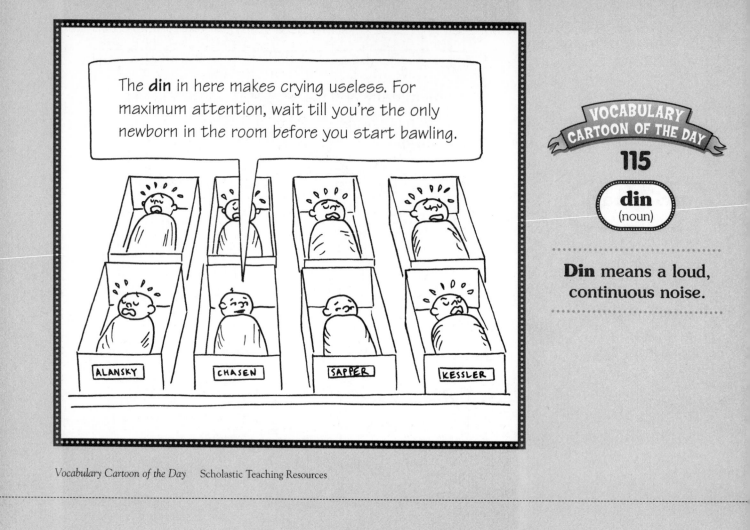

The **din** in here makes crying useless. For maximum attention, wait till you're the only newborn in the room before you start bawling.

ALANSKY   CHASEN   SAPPER   KESSLER

VOCABULARY
CARTOON OF THE DAY

115

din
(noun)

Din means a loud, continuous noise.

I finally found the source of the **incessant** noise you've been hearing, and it's not a ghost.

VOCABULARY
CARTOON OF THE DAY

116

incessant
(adjective)

Something that is **incessant** is continuous without interruption.

117

curb
(verb)

To **curb** means
to control
or restrain.

I'm trying to **curb** my desire to return home right away. I want to enjoy all the free publicity for a little while longer.

BUS
STOP

LOST
DOG

LOST
DOG

LOST
DOG

LOST
DOG

Vocabulary Cartoon of the Day Scholastic Teaching Resources

118

forbear
(verb)

To **forbear** means
to hold back or go
without something.

It's hard to **forbear** when it comes to a second piece of this delicious pie. Are you done with that?

My parents won't **augment** my allowance now that the software I created has sold a million copies.

Vocabulary Cartoon of the Day Scholastic Teaching Resources

119

augment
(verb)

To **augment** means to add on to or increase.

As soon as the sign went up, our customers were quick to **inundate** us with suggestions. The most common has been "Get a box to hold the suggestions."

SUGGESTIONS FOR OUR STORE:

Sale!

120

inundate
(verb)

To **inundate** means to overwhelm or to flood.

Something that is **palpable** can easily be felt.

I've missed the **palpable** tension of the game since they changed the regulation height of the net.

Vocabulary Cartoon of the Day   Scholastic Teaching Resources

Something that is **arcane** is hidden or mysterious.

It's just one of those **arcane** features that every old house has.

You're my big brother. That doesn't mean you're my **prototype**.

VOCABULARY CARTOON OF THE DAY

123

prototype
(noun)

A **prototype** is an original or early version of something on which later versions are based.

Seems like it was just yesterday when I carved this, and already it's **obsolete**.

VOCABULARY CARTOON OF THE DAY

124

obsolete
(adjective)

Something that is **obsolete** is old-fashioned and no longer useful.

125

bristle
(verb)

To **bristle** means to react by showing anger.

The only thing that makes me **bristle** more than seeing the kids track in mud is when I do it myself.

Vocabulary Cartoon of the Day Scholastic Teaching Resources

126

irk
(verb)

To **irk** means to annoy.

If you **irk** your parents by asking for a glass of water every bedtime, you might get one of these, too.

Someone who
is **indefatigable**
is not capable
of being tired out.

Vocabulary Cartoon of the Day   Scholastic Teaching Resources

Tenacity is the
determination to
keep doing what
one believes in.

129

brevity
(noun)

Brevity is the shortness of something.

Vocabulary Cartoon of the Day   Scholastic Teaching Resources

130

copious
(adjective)

Copious means plentiful or containing a large amount.

Four dollars, eleven cents—my talent is the ability to **gauge** how much money is lost in a couch without lifting a cushion.

131

gauge
(verb)

To **gauge** means to guess or estimate the contents or capacity of something.

Earth Day might make the others feel left out. Let's **designate** April 23 as "Rest of the Planets Day."

EARTH DAY
April 22

REST OF THE PLANETS DAY
April 23?

132

designate
(verb)

To **designate** means to choose something for a specific purpose.

133

disseminate
(verb)

When you **disseminate** something, you distribute or spread it around.

134

emanate
(verb)

To **emanate** means to flow out of something.

We don't just **impose** late fines anymore. Now we also give a quiz to make sure you actually read the book you held onto for so long.

PUBLIC LIBRARY

OVERDUE BOOKS ↓

ON TIME BOOKS ↓

135

impose
(verb)

To **impose** means to establish or bring about something by force.

If my mom can take advantage of my filing skills on Take Our Daughters to Work Day, she can **compensate** me in the form of a Take Our Daughters to the Mall Day.

CHESHIRE MALL

VOCABULARY CARTOON OF THE DAY

136

compensate
(verb)

To **compensate** means to make up for something with another thing that's equivalent.

Mom, you've made smart investments for me so far, but I'm feeling **bullish** enough to take over from here.

Vocabulary Cartoon of the Day   Scholastic Teaching Resources

Despite your **tepid** reaction to my science report, I hope you know more about sea cucumbers than you did an hour ago.

VOCABULARY CARTOON OF THE DAY

139

exemplify
(verb)

To **exemplify** means to show or demonstrate by example.

VOCABULARY CARTOON OF THE DAY

140

inimitable
(adjective)

Something that is **inimitable** cannot be imitated or matched.

peruse
(verb)

To **peruse** means
to read carefully.

Vocabulary Cartoon of the Day Scholastic Teaching Resources

digress
(verb)

To **digress** means
to stray or get off
the subject one
was talking or
writing about.

Vocabulary Cartoon of the Day   Scholastic Teaching Resources

propel
(verb)

To **propel** means to move something forward or ahead.

prevail
(verb)

To **prevail** means to succeed or triumph.

A **quota** is the amount or proportion allowed for certain things, such as a place.

The word **droves** refers to a large group, like a crowd.

Breakfast in bed on my birthday brings me **felicity**, but in the future, I'd prefer it on top of the covers.

Vocabulary Cartoon of the Day   Scholastic Teaching Resources

felicity
(noun)

Felicity is another word for happiness.

Why didn't you tell us you had a **qualm** about heights *before* we started on this plan?

FOOD

qualm
(noun)

A **qualm** is a feeling of uneasiness, like being uncomfortable about something.

149

loathe
(verb)

To **loathe** means to dislike strongly or despise.

150

extol
(verb)

To **extol** means to praise highly.

Jim's only in third grade but he's got enough **clout** with the fifth graders to sit at their lunch table.

Clout means influence or power.

Vocabulary Cartoon of the Day   Scholastic Teaching Resources

Maybe he's not a predator. Maybe he's just a mouse **devotee**.

A **devotee** is someone who is a loyal fan or follower.

To **exhort** means to encourage or advise.

To **elude** means to avoid or escape from something.

Please use **discretion** when buying me a birthday present—no toys that clash with the color scheme of my room.

Vocabulary Cartoon of the Day Scholastic Teaching Resources

discretion
(noun)

Discretion means good judgment.

Your **apprehension** is for the wrong reason.

BEWARE OF DOG

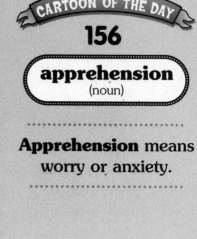

apprehension
(noun)

Apprehension means worry or anxiety.

desolate
(adjective)

Something that
is **desolate** is
empty or lifeless.

Vocabulary Cartoon of the Day Scholastic Teaching Resources

rigorous
(adjective)

Something that is
rigorous is harsh
and very difficult.

A **precedent** is something that has already happened that may be used as an example in dealing with a similar event.

Vocabulary Cartoon of the Day Scholastic Teaching Resources

A **hiatus** is a rest or a break.

161

quiver
(verb)

To **quiver** means
to shake or tremble.

Vocabulary Cartoon of the Day   Scholastic Teaching Resources

162

adhere
(verb)

To **adhere**
means to stick fast,
as if by glue.

Vocabulary Cartoon of the Day   Scholastic Teaching Resources

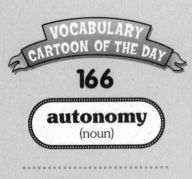

Vocabulary Cartoon of the Day   Scholastic Teaching Resources

Vocabulary Cartoon of the Day   Scholastic Teaching Resources

VOCABULARY CARTOON OF THE DAY

168

condone
(verb)

To **condone** means to overlook or excuse behavior that may be wrong.

VOCABULARY CARTOON OF THE DAY

169

solicit
(verb)

To **solicit** means to call upon or seek by request.

Vocabulary Cartoon of the Day Scholastic Teaching Resources

VOCABULARY CARTOON OF THE DAY

170

bellow
(verb)

To **bellow** means to roar or shout in a deep voice.

Vocabulary Cartoon of the Day   Scholastic Teaching Resources

To **reminisce**
means to fondly
remember something
in the past.

My dad likes to **reminisce** but he's not so good at it. The other day he said, "When I was your age, I was also nine."

Vocabulary Cartoon of the Day Scholastic Teaching Resources

To **divulge**
means to reveal
or make public.

I couldn't **divulge** my secret identity right now even if I wanted to—someone's stepping on my cape.

BUS STOP

Vocabulary Cartoon of the Day Scholastic Teaching Resources

VOCABULARY
CARTOON OF THE DAY

175

assiduous
(adjective)

A person who is
assiduous is very
hardworking and
attentive to details.

VOCABULARY
CARTOON OF THE DAY

176

luminous
(adjective)

Something that
is **luminous** is
shiny and bright.

177

acumen
(noun)

Acumen is another word for expertise or intelligence.

Vocabulary Cartoon of the Day   Scholastic Teaching Resources

178

elation
(noun)

Elation is the state of being happy or filled with joy.

I never stop roasting marshmallows until the last **ember** has died out.

VOCABULARY CARTOON OF THE DAY

179

ember
(noun)

An **ember** is a small, glowing piece of coal or wood.

Vocabulary Cartoon of the Day Scholastic Teaching Resources

I like your **optimism**, but I don't think they'll expand summer vacation to include fall, too.

VOCABULARY CARTOON OF THE DAY

180

optimism
(noun)

Optimism is the belief in good things happening; positive thinking.

Notes